All About

Betty White

Betty White Biography Children's Book for Kids

(With Bonus! Coloring Pages and Videos)

By All About Books

Before You Go Any Further, Get Your FREE Gift! (Worth $67)

Never Fear "The Call" from the School or the Hospital Again!

How to Effectively Communicate With Your Child About *Safety* in a Fun Way!

Did you know if children are not taught properly about safety at a young age, it can potentially lead to reckless, dangerous behaviors even when they become a teenager or an adult?

Never fear "the call" from the school or the hospital with this comprehensive video course!

It'll teach you how to communicate effectively with your young ones about safety without boring them!

(Limited-Time FREE Gift)

Get It Before It Expires Here:

https://allaboutbookseries.com/freegift/

Table of Contents

Disclaimer and Note to Readers:

This book is an unofficial tribute book to Betty White from a fan to support her legacy.

The information in this book is provided for educational and entertainment purposes only.

The information in this book has been compiled from reliable sources. It is accurate to the best of the author's knowledge; however, the author cannot guarantee its accuracy and validity and cannot be held liable for any errors or omissions.

If you use the information contained in this book, you agree that the author is free from and not liable for any damages, costs, and expenses, including any legal fees, potentially resulting from applying any of the information provided by this guide.

The disclaimer applies to any damages or injury caused by the use and application, whether directly or indirectly, of any advice or information presented, whether for breach of contract, tort, neglect, personal injury, criminal intent, or under any other cause of action. You agree to accept all risks of using the information presented inside this book.

If an individual cites this publication as the source of information, it does not imply that the author or publisher endorse the individual or organization's knowledge. This book is an unofficial fan tribute and has not been approved or endorsed by Betty White or her associates.

"Betty White" by Super-Nerd is marked with CC BY-SA 2.0.

Introduction to Betty White

"In a town where comedy rules, Betty White wears the golden crown."

-Betty White Documentary (2018.)

Betty White Ludden is popularly known as "The First Lady of Television." Betty White was a pacesetter and a pioneer; her career is as old as television.

Words cannot express her greatness. She has an honorary title as the 4th mayor of Hollywood. She has a star on the Hollywood Walk of Fame. She has the longest TV career as an entertainer for a female and has a Guinness world record to attest to that as her career spans up to 80 years. She began her career as a comic tactician as far back as the beginning days of television. Endorse the knowledge. Betty is extraordinary to have a career that lasted over eight decades in an industry that depends on youthfulness.

Betty Marion White is a legacy, and we must treat her as such. She was the first woman to ever produce a sitcom. She was also one of the first women to be nominated for an Emmy best actress award; she was the first woman to receive an Emmy award for outstanding game show host for "Just Men." It's so ironic!

She is famous for her roles as Sue Ann Niven in "The Mary Tyler Moore Show," for which she won an Emmy Award, and Rose Nylund in "The Golden Girls."

The entertainer was an avid pet lover, and she is widely known for her advocacy of animals.

White's fame grew because she was authentic in her career. She was effortlessly funny, and she was very much herself. Fans and colleagues widely loved the entertainer for her sass and positivity. She was different from other comics because she had an uncanny ability not just to make a joke but point out the reason behind the gag. As an actress, she could easily make the plainest character be the most loved by finding tricks that merge with the character and delivering them flawlessly. Betty didn't play the character; she embodied the character. What makes it even more spectacular is that Betty White never took an acting class in her life.

She was very dedicated to her work. Her colleagues describe her as having a legendary work ethic; even in her old age, she refused to let her age define her career. She was resourceful and made good use of her old age in her career. She hosted "Saturday Night Live" at the age of 88, "an inspiration to many," I would call her. She continued to show up to work in Hollywood even after many of her generation had retired. She showed us the beauty in old Hollywood as well as contemporary Hollywood. Although Betty belonged to a different era, it didn't deter her acting performance in her old age.

Apart from her excellent acting, Betty was known for her warm personality, kindness, love for animals, advocacy against racial injustice, and support for the LGBTQ+ community.

The entertainer died on December 31, 2021. She was just a few days short of being 100 years old. A lot of Hollywood stars paid tribute to the celebrity. Almost all of them talk about Betty White's kindness.

Matthew Saks, the son of Bea Arthur, mentioned that on the set of "The Golden Girls,"

"Betty would go out and smile and chat with the audience and literally go and make friends with the audience. Which is a nice thing — a lot of them have come from all over the country and are fans."

Betty's kindness radiated to her fans. She took her fan mail seriously and tried to answer personally.

Todd Milliner, the executive producer of "Hot in Cleveland," spoke about Betty's kindness. He said that "Betty's attitude on that stage set a tone from the top down that we all had to be kind and considerate to everybody. I've seen all these social media posts with people sharing memories of Betty White being so kind and so nice. I'm not surprised. Every day she came in thoughtful and considerate and ready to work."

As a result of her hard work, Betty set the pace for entertainers to thrive. Betty's hard work and long career have proven that it's easy to thrive in a space irrespective of your age as long as you work hard.

Betty White's Biography

http://allaboutbookseries.com/BettyWhiteBiography

Betty White's Early Childhood

Betty White grew up in the home of celebrities. On January 17, 1922, Betty White was born in Oak Park, Illinois. She is of Danish, Greek, English, and Welsh descent; impressive.

Her paternal grandfather was Danish, and her maternal grandfather was Greek; her grandmothers were Canadians.

Her parents named her Betty Marion White, not Elizabeth because they didn't like any of the nicknames for Elizabeth.

She was the only child of her parents, Christine Tess and Horace Logan White.

Betty mentioned, "I was the happiest only child that ever walked the face of the earth."

Her mother, Christine Tess (Cachikis), was a homemaker, while her father, Horace Logan White, was a company executive for the Crouse-Hinds Electric Company. He was a war veteran before he married Christine Tess.

Her family moved to Los Angeles during the Great Depression; Betty was two. Her father tried to make extra money by building crystal radios and selling them. However, many people could not afford to pay for radios, so they exchanged them for other goods, including dogs. They ended up with twenty-six dogs.

Betty mentioned that her parents loved animals. Betty joked that she had many four-footed siblings while she was an only child.

Her parents also instilled a great sense of humor in her.

In her book *If You Ask Me*, Betty also mentioned that she learned the art of comedic timing from her parents, which helped her career tremendously.

"I think what helped my comedic timing most were those breakfasts and dinners growing up—I was raised with such funny parents who told marvelous stories; I'd be sitting there as a kid, wanting to add to the conversation, wanting to jump right in with an idea, but if I blurted something out it might ruin the moment. It taught me a lot about the power of waiting."

She attended Horace Mann Elementary school and Beverly Hills High School, both in Beverly Hills.

Betty stated that she had stage fright. It happened the first time in elementary school. She still had it throughout her career as an actress. Talking about her stage fright, Betty said, "You are never calm, but your job is to deliver."

Betty grew up in a version of America where many women were homemakers.

Did you know that Betty White wanted to be a forest ranger? How cool is that? Unfortunately for Betty, women were not allowed to be forest rangers at that time.

Question to Ponder: How do you think Betty felt when she found out that women could not be first rangers? How would you feel when you're not allowed to do something you want?

Betty was interested in wildlife because of her family's vacation trips to the Sierra Nevada. The family spent time together enjoying nature. Betty always looked forward to the last half-day in June when her parents would pick her up early, and they would go camping to enjoy the wildlife.

She also wanted to be a zookeeper but did not fulfill the career. However, she worked with the Los Angeles Zoo for forty-seven years in her later years, thus fulfilling her zookeeper dream. Also, after receiving a letter from the United States Forest Reserve, she was ordained as an honorary forest ranger.

Betty also wanted to be an opera singer. As a result, she was very committed to her singing lessons. The lessons paid off because Betty was a fabulous singer.

Betty began her acting career in elementary school where she wrote and also played the main character in the school's graduation play titled *Land of the Rising Sun*. Throughout high school, she paid a lot of interest in music and drama. She decided to pursue a career in acting.

Her most significant role models are Jeanette MacDonald and Nelson Eddy. They inspired her acting.

Question to Ponder: Do you have any role models? Can you mention them?

Early Career and The World War

Betty started her career in the entertainment industry shortly after graduating high school in 1939. Tragically, no one remembers the title of Betty's debut show on TV, not even Betty. Betty mentioned that it was an experimental work in the Packard building, Downtown LA. She wore her high school graduation dress and sang songs from "The Merry Widow" on the show. She was seventeen.

The experience was exhilarating for Betty; she decided to skip college and actively pursue acting. Her acting debut was at Bliss Hayden Little Theater.

Unfortunately, not long after she began pursuing her acting career, the United States entered the Second World War. Betty joined the American women's voluntary service. Her tasks involved driving a supply truck to Hollywood Hills and participating in entertainment activities for troops before they deployed abroad. One of those events happened to be her debut movie, titled "Time to Kill" (1945), a short film made to educate servicemen about military programs. The cast included Jackie Cooper, George Reeves (who later became MTV's first Superman), DeForest Kelley (who later played the role of Fifty-Eight Bones on *Star Trek*), and Barry Nelson. Wow, Betty was chilling with the big boys.

White, while talking about her wartime service, explained that "It was a strange time and out of balance with everything."

This quote shows how confusing living in a war period can be.

Question to Ponder: How do you think Betty felt about the war? How do you think the war affected Betty and her career?

During the war, Betty met her first husband, Dick Barker, a United States Army Air Forces P-38 pilot. The couple got married after the war and moved to Ohio, where her husband owned a chicken farm. Betty was unhappy in Ohio, so they moved back to Hollywood and divorced within the year. Betty told *People* in a 1999 interview that living on the chicken farm was a "nightmare." Betty White loves animals, so you have to believe her.

Betty's marriage with Dick Barker lasted six months. In a 2010 interview with AARP, Betty revealed why she married Dick Barker. She said, "I would not have married my first husband. I married my first because we wanted to sleep together. It lasted six months, and we were in bed for six months. The marriage with Barker helped me to appreciate the real thing when it came along."

After the war, Betty tried to find work in theaters, but she was not accepted because, according to them, she was not photogenic enough.

Question to Ponder: Have you ever tried to get a role in a school club, but you were turned down for your looks even though you were good enough for the part? How did you feel?

Betty didn't let it deter her. She wanted better for herself, so she began to look for jobs in radio, where being photogenic was not a criterion. She made commercials on the radio for about $5 and would sing on shows for no payment. Some of the shows she starred in include "Blondie," "This Is Your FBI," and "The Great Gildersleeve." She was later offered her show called "The Betty White Show."

Question to Ponder: How do you think Betty must have felt getting her show? How do you feel when your hard work here is rewarded?

In 1947, Betty White married Lane Allen, a Hollywood agent, casting director, and actor. He is famous for his role in the TV series "Police Story" in 1976. The couple split in 1949 because Lane wanted Betty to leave the industry and raise a family, but that did not align with Betty's goals. She was more focused on her career.

Question to Ponder: Have you had a friend who didn't want to play when you wanted? How did you feel knowing that your friend didn't like the same thing as you?

In 1949 Betty White became the co-host of Al Jarvis in his live television show, "Hollywood on Television." Betty and Jarvis performed numerous live advertisements for their sponsors. She once performed fifty-eight live advertisements on the show.

She took over from Jarvis in 1952 after his departure. The show was expanded to five and a half hours a day, six times a week. She was paid $300 weekly.

Betty White's Career in the 1950s

In 1951, she was nominated for her first Emmy Award for Best Actress in a Body of Work, as the award named no shows. She was nominated alongside Judith Anderson, Helen Hayes, Gertrude Berg, and Imogene Coca. Gertrude Berg won the award. This nomination made Betty among the first women to be nominated for an Emmy award. This achievement is iconic and an essential part of history. It goes further to show that Betty White was a pacesetter.

That same year, after she became the host of "Hollywood on TV," Betty went further; she co-founded Handy Productions alongside writer George Tibbles and producer Don Fedderson. They created the TV comedy show "Life with Elizabeth," which won a Los Angeles Emmy Award in 1952. This show made Betty the first woman to produce a sitcom, another achievement of Betty, which is a pivotal moment in television history. The presentation focused on the married life of Elizabeth and her long-suffering husband, Alvin. It would often end with a voice-over asking Elizabeth if it were better if she were ashamed of upsetting her husband, she would sheepishly nod, then the voice-over would call her "stubborn as a mule."

"Life with Elizabeth" was so popular; it allowed Betty to have creative control on camera and behind. Betty could do anything with the show. It was surprising in those days, mainly because the industry was saturated with men. It was more dramatic as she was a twenty-eight-year-old woman who still lived with her parents.

Betty started to host and produce her talk and variety show known as "The Betty White Show" from 1952 to 1954. You might mention that there was a Betty White show before, yes, that's true, but it was for radio. This new Betty White show was for television. The show was a variety show where she would interview guests, read fan mails, and sing with the orchestra.

She featured an African American tap dancer as a member of the cast in this new show. This act led to many criticisms, significantly when the show expanded nationally. Betty ignored the complaints and gave the tap dancer, Arthur Duncan, more air time. Local stations in the southern states threatened to snub the show. The threat by local stations was a blatant display of racism and racial segregation. In response, Betty told them to "live with it." It affected the performance, which led to lower viewership and cancellation of the show. Betty never told Arthur Duncan what happened on the show. This proved to be a significant and compelling part of Betty White's career.

Question to Ponder: How do you think racial segregation affected "The Betty White Show"? If you were Betty, would you have taken Arthur Duncan, the African American tap dancer, off the show?

In 1957, after the finale of "Life with Elizabeth," Betty starred as Vicki Angel on ABC's sitcom, "Date with the Angels." "The show was a disaster." White mentioned,

Question to Ponder: Have you ever felt like you needed to get out of doing a particular work because you didn't like how it was going?

Unfortunately for Betty, there was no getting out of the contract as ABC refused to release her. To fulfill the thirteen weeks left on her contract, she went for a reboot of her old show, "The Betty White Show." The show aired till the end of her contract. The new Betty White show was a comedy variety show which lasted fourteen episodes. One positive experience that came out of it was that Betty met Lucille Ball and they became best of friends. Their friendship was so strong that it extended to their husbands. They were best friend couples. Betty mentioned in the cheat sheet in 2014. "Lucy was one of my dearest friends ... She was dynamite. Everything you saw was what you got."

Betty also mentioned that while they never worked together, it felt like they did because they were always hanging out as buddies. The friendship also extended to their mothers. And when Lucy lost her mother, she took Tess White as her mother.

Betty White; 1960s First Lady of Game Shows

Betty White started to make frequent game show appearances; in the 1960s, she was a famous face. She also appeared on talk shows. She appeared in "The Tonight Show" with Jack Paar and Johnny Carson. She made many appearances on "The Password," where she met the love of her life, Allen Ludden. She was a regular panelist on match games. She also made appearances on "What's My Line?" "To Tell the Truth," and other spin-offs of "Password."

NBC proposed a job for her as the anchor of their breakfast show "Today." Betty declined because she did not want to move to New York, the studio's location.

Question to Ponder: Have you ever had to move to a new city for one reason or another? How did it feel knowing you were leaving your friends?

NBC sweetened the offer for Betty. They offered her an apartment at St Regis Hotel and offered to fly her into New York weekly to do the show. However, Betty turned down the offer. She said that it was not worth it or practical when she considered the time spent traveling. Barbara Walters got the job.

She hosted the annual Rose Parade broadcast on NBC for nineteen years. She co-hosted with Roy Neal and later Lorne Greene. Betty White began hosting the Macy's Thanksgiving parade alongside Lorne Greene. The duo continued to host till 1972.

In 1963, she married Allen Ludden. In an interview with closer weekly in 2017, Betty said, "I wish I didn't have two bad marriages. They were probably my fault. I just didn't marry the right men. … I had lovely relationships, but not anything in the league of Allen."

Betty has mentioned that she regrets not getting married to Ludden earlier. She was hesitant about marrying Ludden because of her previously failed marriages. Also, she was in a relationship at that time, and she didn't want to move to New York, where Ludden hosted his show. Also, Ludden lost his wife around that period.

She rejected his engagement ring, and he wore it on his neck till she agreed. She had admitted to herself that she didn't want to live the rest of her life without Ludden, so she agreed to his proposal. Betty mentioned that the ring had tan lines by the time she decided. They got married in Las Vegas, with Betty's parents present.

Question to Ponder: Have you ever been scared to do something? How did you get over it?

The actress also told Piers Morgan in 2018 that "I had 18 wonderful years with Allen Ludden. … The first two were rehearsals."

Betty was with Allen Ludden till his death in 1981 from stomach cancer. She refused to remarry after Luden's death. In her words, "When you've had the best, what's left?" She never had children; she was happy with Allen's children and her entertainment career.

Betty White Talks About Her Relationship with Allen Ludden on The Joan Rivers Show

http://allaboutbookseries.com/BettyWhiteAllenLudden

Betty's Career in the 1970s

While Betty had her film debut in 1962, in the film "Advise and Consent," where she played the role of Senator Elizabeth Ames Adams, a Kansas senator, the 1970s came with more opportunities for the entertainer to showcase her skills.

In 1971, Betty hosted a show called "The Pet Set." The show featured celebrities and their pets. It was produced by her husband and lasted just one season. It ended when Carnation pulled out its advertising.

Between 1973 and 1974, Betty appeared several times on the fourth season of "The Mary Tyler Moore Show." She played the character of Sue Ann Nivens. The sickeningly sweet and perfect character in "the happy homemaker" was sarcastic, cynical, man-obsessed, and competitive. She portrayed the role brilliantly.

The show needed someone sickeningly sweet like Betty, so she was auditioned. The producers were skeptical because of her friendship with Mary Tyler Moore; they were scared that things would get awkward if Betty White didn't fit the part.

Question to Ponder: Have you ever been in a position where you almost did not get a chance to do something because of your friends? How did you feel?

However, Betty White played that role and did justice to it, and by the fifth season, she was a permanent member of the cast. Sue Ann Nivens had an affair with Lars Lindstrom, the dermatologist husband of Phyllis Lindstrom. This leads to a clash between Phyllis and Sue Ann when introduced as WJM's "Happy Homemaker." Their colleagues try to prevent them from running into one another.

Betty's role earned her three Emmy nominations, and she won two.

Betty White's Wins an Emmy for Her Role as Sue Anne Nivens

http://allaboutbookseries.com/BettyWhiteWinsEmmySueAnneNivens

In 1975, Betty White lost her job as the commentator hostess of the Tournament of Roses Parade. NBC felt that she was too closely associated with their rival network CBS's "The Mary Tyler Moore Show." It was a trying time for Betty as she has admitted that watching someone else do the parade she loved hosting was difficult.

Question to Ponder: How do you think Betty White felt about losing her job as the commentator hostess of the Tournament of Rose Parade? Recall an incident where you lost something you loved.

Happy days will always come around. That's why after the "Mary Tyler Moore Show" ended in 1977, Betty was given her show, "The Betty White Show"; she co-starred with John Hillerman and Georgia Engel, her former co-star in the Mary Tyler Moore show. This new Betty White Show was a sitcom that featured the life of an actress in a fictional cop show. The actress Joyce, whom Betty White plays, lands the role of the lead character in an undercover police show. She is thrilled about the show till she learns that the director of the show is her ex-husband, played by John Hillerman. Georgia Engel plays the role of her naive best friend and roommate.

Unfortunately, this show shared the same time slot as "Monday Night Football." The show had poor ratings, so it was canceled after a season.

Betty was a guest star in a lot of mini-series, including "With This Ring," "The Best Place to Be," " Before and After," and "The Gossip Columnist."

"Betty White" by Alan Light is marked with CC BY 2.0.

Betty White's Career in the 1980s: The Golden Girls

In 1981, Betty lost her husband, Allen Ludden, to stomach cancer. It was difficult for the actress, but she bounced back and buried herself in work. Fans started to speculate that she had reached the peak of her career. Unknown to them, Betty White was just getting started.

Betty had recurring appearances in game shows and talk shows. She was bringing the spice to those shows. In 1984, she won a daytime Emmy Award as the outstanding Gameshow Host. She became the first woman to win this award for the NBC game show "Just Men." This is so ironic it makes me laugh. As a result of her hard work and dedication to these game shows, she was crowned "The First Lady of Game Shows."

She had the honor of starring in "Mama's Family" alongside Rue McClanahan in 1983. The show is a spin-off from "The Carol Burnett Show." Betty played the role of Ellen Harper, the snobbish elder sister of Eunice Harper. The sisters had their unhealthy dose of sibling rivalry. This was further fueled by Ellen's ability to do things right. She was their mother's favorite child; despite this, she is also a victim of her mother's criticism, insults, and wrath. This is slightly different from her character in "The Carol Burnett Show," as Ellen Harper would often snap back at their mother.

Before the end of the series, she got her second hit role as Rose Nylund in "The Golden Girls." She starred alongside Bea Arthur, Estelle Getty, and Rue McClanahan. The show was about four widowed or divorced women in their golden years, hence, the title. These women shared a home in Miami. The show was so successful it ran from 1985 till 1992. Betty won an Emmy award for outstanding actress in a comedy in the show's first season due to her role. She was nominated as a supporting actress throughout the show's run every year. In the years following "The Golden Girls," Betty made $3 million yearly on returns.

It is no rumor that Betty had a strained relationship with her co-star, Bea Arthur. Betty mentioned that Bea Arthur "was not that fond of me...she found me a pain in the neck sometimes. It was my positive attitude, and that made Bea mad sometimes. Sometimes if I were happy, she'd be furious."

Question to Ponder: Have you ever worked with someone who didn't like you? How did you cope?

While they didn't have a great personal relationship, both actresses respected one another and the show. The show was level ground for both actresses. Their differences did not matter; what mattered was the show, their roles, and all that they had set to achieve with the show. As viewers of the show, it is so hard to believe that they didn't have a good relationship in real life. They had great chemistry on the show; it was hard to believe otherwise.

When Bea Arthur died in 2009, Betty was sad; she said, "I knew it would hurt; I just didn't know it would hurt this much."

Todd Milliner, the executive producer of "Hot in Cleveland," mentioned in his tribute to Betty White that the only time they ever saw Betty sad on stage was after she heard the news of Bea Arthur's demise.

One fun fact about the "Golden Girls" is that Betty was offered the role of Blanche, and Rue McClanahan was offered the position of Rose. The parts provided to these stars were similar to some of their previous roles. The director told both of them to switch roles since they had played similar roles previously. The Director feared that viewers would see Betty White play the role of Blanche and just think, "She's Sue Ann in another guise."

Question to Ponder: Have you ever been told not to do a part because you had played that part before?

Rue McClanahan mentioned in a documentary that Betty was confused about the character of Rose.

Question to Ponder: Have you ever been confused about the work you were supposed to do? How did it feel not to understand the work?

Betty White was not happy about it, and she was taken aback. The director mentioned that *"Rose was the trickiest character to play because she is vague."*

However, the director Joe Sandrich mentioned that Rose was terminally naive. Then white joked, "If you told Rose you were so hungry you could eat a horse; she'd call the ASPCA."

Excuse me, but that was a perfect joke. It portrays Betty's ability to find a joke based on a character and deliver it flawlessly.

The writer of the series wrote the character of Rose to be the butt of the joke. Every time, she gave the perfect comeback from each insult or misunderstanding, ready to strike again. White's delivery of Rose's character conveyed a sort of obtuse cluelessness, and underneath this cluelessness hid a savage intelligence. Rose often won their verbal arguments with her unexpected delivery, which always had perfect timing. She knew when to strike.

http://allaboutbookseries.com/BettyWhiteinGoldenGirls

In 1987, Betty White published her first book "Betty White In Person." Betty talks about her life as a closet writer. She portrays her love for animals by asking for support for local zoos and animal shelters from her colleagues. She talks about her "Golden Girls" colleagues and how they keep her sane. She talks about her late husband, too. She mentions how she dislikes sloppy diction, mirrored sunglasses, blatant sex, and voyeurism on today's TV. The tempo of the book was very bubbly and filled with positivity. She also spoke about her book on the John Carson show, where she was very entertaining.

Betty White Talks About Betty White in Person

http://allaboutbookseries.com/BettyWhiteAboutBettyWhite

Betty White's Career in the 1990s

After the Golden girls ended in 1992, Betty starred in "The Golden Palace" with Rue McClanahan and Estelle Getty. This is after Bea Arthur leaves the cast of "The Golden Girls." The series lasts just one season.

She also played the role of "Rose Nylund" as a guest star in "Suddenly Susan," "The Practice," and "Yes, Dear."

She published her second book in 1995 titled *Here I Go Again: My Life In Television*. This is a memoir talking about Betty's career from her first show. We look behind the scene into Betty White's entertainment career; we go back in time from her time on radio till the 1990s. The memoir talks about many things that Betty did in her life. Her humor and positivity radiate all through the book.

She got nominated for Emmy awards severally.

She also won a primetime Emmy award for Outstanding Guest Actress in a Comedy Series. She appeared as herself on an episode of "The John Larroquette Show" in 1996. In the episode, "Here We Go Again," In a total Betty-like manner, she tells the host John Larroquette to assist her in writing her memoir. The episode gets more interesting when they talk about her role as Rose Nylund. Larroquette reads a script about Rose Nylund's lines in the series. He talks about how hard it was to focus, with Betty White giving him her full attention.

Larroquette discusses how the other girls used to have big laughs, too. Betty White says the crew manufactured the laughs. Things get juicier when her Golden Girls co-stars, Rue McClanahan and Estelle Getty, join the show. Larroquette was forced to dress up as a drag Bea Arthur, and the four of them emerge as the original Golden Girls. It was hilarious. Going back to that episode, it is no surprise that Betty won an award for that episode.

Betty White in the John Laroquette Show

http://allaboutbookseries.com/BettyWhiteinJohnLarroquetteShow

Question to Ponder: How do you feel when you win medals?

In 1998, she appeared in the *Dennis the Menace* movie. She plays the character of Martha Wilson, George Wilson's wife, who dotes on Dennis. She gives him a lot of cookies and milk. She's usually Stern with George when he's harsh to Dennis.

In 1999, she starred in "Ladies Man" as the mother of a single father, Alfred Molina. She appeared for two seasons.

She also starred in "Lake Placid" in 1999. She plays the role of Delores Bickerman, an elderly widow who feeds the mutant crocodile and treats it as a pet.

Betty White in the 2000s

Betty appeared in a series of TV series in the early 2000s. In 2005 she played the role of scheming blackmailer, Catherine Piper, in "Boston Legal." She had initially played this role as a guest star in "The Practice."

In December 2006, she joined the cast of "The Bold and the Beautiful," taking the part of Ann Douglas. Her role as Ann Douglas, the mother of the show's matriarch, Stephanie Forrester, was profound. Betty's taking this role came as a surprise to fans because it is different from her usual comedic roles. Ann was so fixated on having a perfect life; she denied that her husband abused her elder daughter. Even when her younger daughter Pamela spoke about the abuse, she claimed they were exaggerating her husband's discipline of his daughter. She later confessed that she knew about the abuse but was too afraid to call out her husband.

Betty portrayed the role of Ann Douglas beautifully. Her portrayal of the role further proved her brilliance as an actress. She appeared on the show till the character's death.

As a talk show and game show goddess, she appeared in more talk shows like "The Tonight Show with Jay Leno" and "The Late Late Show with Craig Ferguson."

She was also a guest star on a remake of the game show "Password" known as "Million Dollar Password." She participated in the Million Dollar challenge at the end of the show.

She also appeared on "The Oprah Winfrey Show" as one of the guests for "The Mary Tyler Moore Show" reunion special alongside every surviving cast member.

In 2006, animal lover Betty had a stellar experience. She was honored with a plaque next to the Gorilla exhibit at the LA Zoo. She was named Ambassador to the Animals.

In 2007, She was spotlighted in television commercials for PetMed Express, expressing her concern for animal welfare.

She also starred in "The Proposal (2009)" alongside Ryan Reynolds and Sandra Bullock. Ryan Reynolds was one of her great friends till she died. She plays the role of Grandma Annie, Andrew Paxton's grandmother. Andrew Paxton is played by Ryan Reynolds. Grandma Annie is funny and kind-hearted. It sounds like a legend we know. Real-life Betty is also known for her kindness. She charmed her co-actors in the movie. Till her death, Sandra Bullock and Ryan Reynolds still competed over who loved Betty most.

In 2009, she was in the Mars campaign alongside Abe Vigoda. The candy company's campaign slogan was "You're not you when you're hungry." The commercial shows Betty playing football. She was hit in the game, then a player huffs: "You're playing like Betty White out there!"

"That's not what your girlfriend says," she retorts, playing off her sweet, yet salty, fashion. (Ouch) that burns.

She's given a bar of Snickers, and she transforms into an agile young man. She starts to dribble, then one of the players turns into Abe Vigoda.

The commercial became famous as it was the company's commercial for the 2010 Super Bowl XLIV. It topped the Super Bowl Ad Meter.

Betty White Snickers Ad

http://allaboutbookseries.com/BettyWhiteSnickersAd

Betty told Times in 2010, "It's so ridiculous at my age to have all this going on; I'm loving it." Betty was given the Screen Actors Guild honorary award for Lifetime Achievement.

Betty's Career Rejuvenation

The Super Bowl ad was a huge success; it pushed Betty's career up. It's safe to say that the entertainer never really went away from television. She was the perfect guest on talk shows and game shows. The Snickers ad did magic for her career, but she never really left TV.

Not long after the ad aired, the actress' fans on Facebook started to make a campaign. They called it "Betty White to Host SNL (please)." David Matthews pioneered the Facebook campaign.

The movement began in January 2010 and was almost at half a million members when NBC verified that she would host "Saturday Night Live" in May 2010. This made Betty the oldest person to host the "Saturday Night Live" show. She was 88 when she made her appearance on the show. A fun fact about this is that Betty White had been previously asked to host "Saturday Night Live," and she rejected it three times.

Betty joked that she, "didn't know what Facebook was, and now that she knows what it is, she had to admit that it sounds like a massive waste of time."

She also joked about the show being a live show. She said, "I'm not new to live TV…Of course, back then, we didn't want to do it live. We just didn't know how to tape things. So I don't know what this show's excuse is."

And, of course, Betty White delivered brilliantly; She won a 2010 Primetime Emmy Award for Outstanding Guest Actress in a Comedy Series.

Talking about the show, Betty spoke about how they used cue cards and teleprompters, and she didn't want to do that because she didn't want to take her eyes off the camera. She was scared she was not going to do it well. So, the person holding the cue cards told her to focus on him, Betty did that with hesitancy, but it worked.

She also mentioned that after each sketch in "Saturday Night Live," someone drags you and rips your clothes, while "someone else is touching your makeup and yet someone else is removing your wig and pinning a new one,(ouch) your hand is grabbed again to drag you on stage and your too frazzled to remember which sketch is next until you get back to those blessed cue cards." Betty mentioned that all she did was glare at her agent, Jeff Witjas; she had to admit it was an exciting experience. When she was asked about it, she said it was not something she would do again.

Later in June, Betty White got the role of Elka Ostrovsky, the old caretaker on TV Land's first original sitcom, "Hot in Cleveland," along with Valerie Bertinelli, Jane Leeves, and Wendie

Malick. The series centers on three aging industry veterans, Melanie Hope Moretti, Rejoyla "Joy" Scroggs, and Victoria Chase. They decide to stay in the city of Cleveland, Ohio, when their plane makes an emergency landing. In Hollywood, you're as relevant as how young you are. So, when these women get a lot of attention in Cleveland, they decide they are not leaving.

They lease a house from Elka Ostrovsky, who still lives in the guest house. Initially, Betty was supposed to stay in the first episode, but they told her to wait till the end of the show, which lasted six seasons and 128 episodes.

In her book *If You Ask Me,"* Betty wrote about how she tried to reject the role because her schedule was packed. She told her agent, "'No, Jeff, that wasn't the agreement. My schedule hasn't let up. I don't know how I could possibly do it!' Here I should mention that the taping schedule for a television series is four or five days a week, requiring me to be on set sometimes for 10 hours a day! Much as I love the show and the company, I'm still on overload. There's no room whatsoever to work in a series! P.S. Guess who signed on for all 20 episodes? I have the backbone of a jellyfish."

In Betty White Fashion, Elka is hilarious; she's direct and opinionated. The actress gives an excellent performance, from running jokes about her age to talking about how she doesn't like "Joy" in the show. She always has a biting remark ready to roll off her tongue, especially when it comes to joy. She has more dating games than the three younger ladies. She seems to have fun with her boyfriend, played by Carl Reiner.

At this point, it is clear that Betty is a legend. It doesn't matter how old she is; she is still oozing talent.

Todd Milliner, the producer of "Hot in Cleveland," said about Betty's performance in the series that Betty "was all-in; She was game for everything...She was a generous performer...Everybody adored her and her talent. There was never a complaint about Betty."

She was nominated for a primetime Emmy as Outstanding Supporting Actress in a Comedy Series for her role as Elka but lost the award.

However, Betty White won two Screen Actors Guild for her role as Elka in the comedy. Betty mentioned that she was amazed when she won the award, but her co-stars were very excited. She said she really wanted the series to win an award, but everyone was so happy with her award that it didn't matter.

She also starred in the Hallmark Hall of Fame presentation of "The Lost Valentine." This presentation won first place in the prime time slot for that date. It also has the highest Hallmark Hall of Fame presentation rating compared to the preceding four years. The presentation won her a nomination for a Screen Actors Guild for her role.

She was the host and executive producer of "Betty White's Off Their Rockers," a show where senior citizens pranked youths. The show went on from 2012 to 2014, and she earned three Emmy nominations.

http://allaboutbookseries.com/BettyWhiteOffTheirRockers

She launched her clothing line in 2010, which featured shirts with her face on them. The sales proceeded to various animal charities that she supported.

In 2011, she starred in a commercial for a life insurance company with British rapper Luciana. In the video, they remix Luciana's song "I'm Still Hot." The video won awards for best branding social media video and best viral video campaign. It topped the Billboard chart for dance club hits in2011.

In 2012, she won a Grammy. It was her first time winning a Grammy. It was an Award for Best Spoken Word Recording for her bestseller "If You Ask Me."

"If you ask me- and of course, you won't; Betty White talks about friendship, romantic love, aging, television, fans, love for animals, and being a celebrity.

In the recording, Betty shares a lifetime of lessons and advice. It feels like your grandmother is in the room, having a chat with you about random events in her life. It's hilarious and honest; it gives more insight into the legend's life: Betty White.

First, I have to agree with her when she says;

"If one has no sense of humor, one is in trouble."

She also talks about life lessons.

"You don't luck into integrity. You work at it."

Talking about Animals, Betty said she prefers animals to people because "Animals don't lie. Animals don't criticize. If animals have moody days, they handle them better than humans do."

The actress seemed to love growing older. She said, "It's old age, not a surprise; we knew it was coming – make the most of it. So you may not be as fast on your feet, and the image in your mirror may be a little disappointing, but if you are still functioning and not in pain, gratitude should be the name of the game."

She also mentioned that you're as old as you feel.

Betty spoke about her love for puzzles; she uses them as a mental exercise. She mentioned that her memory makes her climb the stairs a lot which is all the exercise she needs. And she takes a cocktail before dinner.

She spoke about her autograph. She mentioned how her colleagues tried to always make everything fancy. She wanted to start practicing her autograph.

She spoke about Robert Redford. The entertainer has publicly mentioned that she has a crush on Robert Redford. She mentioned how starstruck she was when she got a letter congratulating her for winning a screen actor's Guild. She admitted that she first thought that someone was trying to play a prank on her, but she saw the signature.

Question to Ponder: How would you feel if you got a letter from your crush? How do you think Betty felt?

The crew of "Hot in Cleveland " tried to get Robert Redford to work with them because of Betty, but it never happened. Yeah, Betty White and Robert Redford were never on television together.

The tempo is that of your grandmother chatting with you about her daily life and the life lessons you should learn from her. The audiobook, in the usual Betty White fashion, is fun.

You're listening to Betty recount different aspects of her life, and you just can't stop laughing. There is so much wisdom there.

Betty talks about her parents and her late husband, Allen Ludden. She talks about friends she made in the industry and her fans.

She spoke about her health; she mentioned how her eyes were not as good as when she was younger, and her memory was not as sharp.

She mentions how her fans always turn her trip to the airport into a meet and greet. She comments about missing a flight once due to the influx of fans at the airport. However, she is grateful for them.

Question to Ponder: Have you ever been late because one of your favorite people delayed you? How did you feel?

She also won the UCLA Jack Benny Award for Comedy; the award recognized her substantial contribution to comedy in television.

Betty's 90th birthday celebration was a big affair. It was aired on NBC the day before her birthday, January 16, 2012. It featured many stars with whom she had worked over the last seventy years of her career. There was a message from the sitting US President, Barack Obama.

Betty was a guest star on WWE Raw, which earned her a Slammy award for Raw guest star of the year.

In 2015, Betty White made her final appearance on "Saturday Night Live" when she attended the 40th Anniversary Special. She participated in "The Californians" sketch with Bill Hader, Taylor Swift, and Kerry Washington. She kissed Bradley Cooper at the end of the sketch.

Betty White also won an honorary Emmy Award for lifetime achievement in 2015.

Betty White: First Lady of Television

Betty's career was celebrated in 2018 with a PBS documentary. It was filmed over ten years. It featured interviews with friends and colleagues.

In Pixar's *Toy Story 4* (2019), Betty was the voice of Bitey White, a toy tiger named after her. The other toys were named after and played by Carl Reiner, Carol Burnett, and Mel Brooks.

Betty said that she loved the way they incorporated their names with that of the animals.

Betty White has always mentioned that she was the "luckiest broad on two feet" to have had a career as long as she did.

Question to Ponder: What do you love doing most? How do you feel about doing it?

Betty White's Death

The world was shocked on December 31, 2021, when Betty White's longtime agent and friend Jeff Witjas confirmed her death. Betty died in her home in North Carmelina Avenue in the Brentwood neighborhood of Los Angeles. The Los Angeles Police Department confirmed that her death was of natural causes. However, the death certificate issued by LA County states that Betty Marion Ludden (she took her husband's name) died of a cerebrovascular accident. In simple terms, Betty White died from a stroke. A stroke occurs when blood flow is lost to a part of the brain. It was revealed that the stroke occurred six days before her death on Christmas Day.

She was cremated the following day, and Glenn Kaplan, who was entrusted with carrying out her advanced health care directive

Her death is saddening to both her human friends and her friends from the animal kingdom. Ryan Reynolds said Betty was old, but she didn't feel old enough.

Her agent also said that he often thought Betty would live forever.

Betty White mentioned in 2012 that she was not afraid of death. She told Bruni of *People* that her mother had an excellent approach to death. "She always thought of it as — We know we have managed to find out almost anything that exists, but nobody knows ... what happens at that moment when it's over. It's the one secret that we don't know. So whenever we would lose somebody very close and very dear, she would always say, 'Well, now he knows the secret.' And it took the curse off of it somehow."

Betty knows the secret now.

Betty White lived a happy life, and millions of people loved her. They expressed it by always visiting her on set. Many times, they came along with their pets. Her fans also sent letters till her death.

Betty White will be remembered for her love for her job as an entertainer. She often talked about how much she loved her job. In her defense, she claimed that there was no point doing it if she didn't love her job.

It is rumored that she left a generous sum to her favorite animal charities. However, it is said that her dogs will get the best. The entertainer allegedly ensured her will stipulated they have luxury collars and leashes. Plus, their valet and housekeeper.

Following her death, millions of people have continued to pay tribute to the actress, including Joe Biden, the current president of The United States. He wrote, "Betty White brought a smile to the lips of generations of Americans. She's a cultural icon who will be sorely missed. Jill and I are thinking of her family and all those who loved her this New Year's Eve."

Ryan Reynolds, Betty's friend and co-star in the 2009 romantic comedy "The Proposal," wrote, "The world looks different now. She was great at defying expectations. She managed to grow very old and, somehow, not old enough. We'll miss you, Betty. Now you know the secret."

Question to Ponder: How do you think Betty would feel about all the nice things people have to say about her?

Tribute to Betty White

http://allaboutbookseries.com/RememberingBettyWhite

Betty White's Awards and Achievement

Betty White has won a lot of awards in her lifetime. It's an accolade for her outstanding work as an entertainer.

Betty White didn't end her acting and comedic career without achieving so many great feats that would leave her mouth hanging. Throughout the course of her career, she was nominated for various awards fifty-seven times and won twenty-seven times.

Betty White won an award in every decade for which she worked; it is such an outstanding feat. She's the only woman to have received an Emmy in all comedic performing categories. Amazing, isn't it? Betty White is a trailblazer.

All of Betty White's Nominations for various Awards are listed below;

● She was nominated for the American Comedy Awards four times and won three times

● She was nominated for the Britannia Awards once and won it.

● She was nominated for The Comedy Award once.

● She was nominated for The Disney Legends Awards once and won it.

- She was nominated for the Primetime Emmy Awards twenty-one times and won it five times.

- She was nominated for the Daytime Emmy Awards twice and won once.

- She was nominated for the Regional Emmy Awards once and won it.

- She was nominated for the Gracie Allen Awards once and won it.

- She was nominated for the Grammy Awards once and won it.

- She won the Golden Apple Award without a nomination.

- She was nominated for the Golden Globe Award four times.

- She was nominated for the MTV Movie Award twice.

- She was nominated for the NewNowNext Award once.

- She was nominated for the People's Choice Award twice and won it once.

- She was nominated for the Screen Actors Guild Awards five times and won it two times.

- She was nominated for the Slammy Award once.

- She was nominated for the Teens Choice Award once and won it.

- She was nominated for the TV Land Award four times and won it all four times.

- She was nominated for the UCLA Jack Benny Award once and won it.

- She was nominated for the VQT "Q" Award two times and won it two times.

- She was nominated for the Women Film Critics Circle Award once and won it once.

Out of the fifty-seven nominations Betty White received, she won a total of twenty-seven awards, and all the awards she won are mentioned below in order of their categories.

Betty White has the longest gap between her first Emmy nomination and her Last Emmy nomination; her first was in 1951, and her last in 2014.

Her American Comedy Awards include

- Funniest female performer in a tv series (The Golden Girls) - Year 1987

- Lifetime achievement award in comedy - Year 1990

- Funniest female guest appearance in a TV series (Ally McBeal) - Year 2000

Her Britannia Award Include;

• Charlie Chaplin Britannia Award for Excellence in Comedy - Year 2010

In The Comedy Awards, she won

• Best Actress in a TV Comedy (Hot in Cleveland) - Year 2011

In the Disney Legends Awards, she won

• Disney Legend - Year 2009

Her Primetime Emmy Awards include

• Outstanding supporting actress in a comedy series - Year 1975 and 1976

• Outstanding lead actress in a comedy series (The Golden Girls) - Year 1986

• Outstanding guest actress in a comedy series (The John Larroquette Show) - Year 1996

• Outstanding guest actress in a comedy series (Saturday Night Live) - 2010

Her Daytime Emmy awards include

- Outstanding game show host for Just Men in Year 1983

- She was also honored a lifetime achievement in 2015

Her Regional Emmy Award include

- Los Angeles Emmy Award for Outstanding Personality (Life with Elizabeth) - Year 1952

Her Gracie Allen Award includes

- Best Actress in a comedy series in Hot in Cleveland - 2011

Her Grammy Award includes

- Best spoken word recording for "If You Ask Me -And Of Course You Won't" - 2011

Her Golden Apple Award includes

- Female star of the year 1986

She won TV icon in 2015 in the People's Choice Awards

Her Screen Actors Awards include

- Outstanding Performance by a Female Actor in a comedy series for "Hot in Cleveland" - Year 2011

- Outstanding Performance by a Female Actor in a comedy series for "Hot in Cleveland" - Year 2012

She has an honorary Screen Actors Guild award for

- Lifetime Achievement Award in 2010

Her Teen Choice Award includes

- Best Dance for The Proposal in 2010

Her TV Land Awards include

- Quintessential Non-Traditional Family award in The Golden Girls- Year 2003

- Groundbreaking Show in The Mary Tyler Moore Show - Year 2004

- Pop Culture Award in The Golden Girls - 2008

- Legendary Award - 2015

She won a UCLA Jack Benny Award as a comedian in 2011

Her Awards for Viewers for Quality TV "Q" includes

● Best Actress in a Quality Comedy Series ("The Golden Girls") - Year 1987

● Best Actress in a Quality Comedy Series ("The Golden Girls") - Year 1988

She won a Life Achievement Award under the Women Film Critics Circle Award in 2021

She has a Star on the Walk of Fame under the Hollywood Walk of Fame in 1995

2010 Betty White Screen Actors Guild Lifetime Achievement Award

http://allaboutbookseries.com/BettyWhiteSAG2010

Betty White's Day

Another of her achievements is that after her death, given her legacy, the legislative arm in her home state of Illinois passed a resolution declaring January 17, 2022, to be Betty White's day.

File:Betty White 2010.jpg" by David Shankbone is marked with CC BY 2.0.

Betty White's Advocacy for Animals

Betty White's advocacy for animals is an award-worthy act that created a legacy for her in her 99 years of living. She supported non-profit organizations and advocated for a better and more improved animal welfare system. It was evident from her lifestyle that she dedicated a greater part of her life not only to the entertainment world but also to help animals and improve their welfare since 1971.

Betty White was closely involved with the Morris Animal Foundation, a non-profit organization that focused on how to improve the lives of animals and also reduce non-human animal diseases. In the course of this journey, she took various positions for over forty years.

It is a known fact that Betty White loved animals. The actress donated to a lot of charities for animals. She also spoke about how fans would bring their dogs to her movie set to pet them. She loved it.

Betty White once turned down a role in "As Good as it Gets" because there was a scene of animal cruelty. In the film, one of the characters throws a dog down a laundry chute.

"When I read the part, I told the director, James Brooks, 'I just can't do that! I know it's for laughs, but given my feelings about animals and my work for animal welfare, I just didn't find it funny. I didn't think it would be a good example to people who might try it in real life."

Betty has expressed that she had no regrets about rejecting the role.

Question to Ponder: What do you think of Betty rejecting the role in the movie? Do you think it is nice that a dog was thrown down the laundry chute for people to laugh?

In 2010, she established the Betty White Wildlife fund through the Morris Animal Foundation in response to the severe oil spill that affected a great number of marine life. And till today, in honor of her wishes, the fund continues to address wildlife health issues.

Also, while working with the American Humane Organization, Betty White was awarded the non-profit's National Humanitarian Medal, which is a lifetime achievement as a result of her honest and total dedication to the cause.

Furthermore, in 2009, Betty was awarded the Jane Goodall Institute Global leadership award, another lifetime achievement as a result of her continuous contribution for decades to protecting wildlife again.

Also noteworthy is the fact that Betty made a great lot of donations, both openly and anonymously, to save animals. One widely known is her donation of seventy thousand dollars to evacuate Penguins and otters after a hurricane put their lives in danger.

Not long after Betty White's death, in honor of her 100th birthday, her supporters kept her dream active and started a #Bettywhitechallenge on Twitter and later on various social media platforms. The challenge involved people donating to any animal shelter or rescue of their choice. This commenced on January 17, 2022.

Betty White's Advocacy for the LGBTQ+ Community

Betty White, a great icon, was known for her comical abilities and love for animals and had a strong standing in her support for her fans in the LGBTQ+ community. In an interview, when she was questioned on the rights of those from the LGBTQ+ community, Betty said, *"Oh, I don't care who you sleep with, whom you sleep with, it's what kind of a human being you are."* She couldn't phantom why people were against the LGBTQ+ community; as she said, "It's such a personal, private business and none of mine."

Betty was also strongly in support of same-sex marriage, and in an interview with Parade, she expressed her opinion that gays should have a right to marry. She went on to state that "I don't care who anybody sleeps with. If a couple has been together all that time, and there are gay relationships that are more solid than some heterosexual ones, I think it's fine if they want to get married. I don't know how people can get so anti-something. Mind your own business, take care of your affairs, and don't worry about other people so much."

Noteworthy is the fact that Betty White didn't only support the LGBTQ+ community, but she also did show her support in 2013 by changing her name along with her other Hot in Cleveland co-stars to *Betty Purple* for a day to celebrate the spirit day, an anti-LGBTQ+ bullying awareness day.

Also, when a female character in the popular TV show, The Golden Girls, showed interest in Betty's character, instead of mocking such a character, the show embraced the idea of lesbianism. This showed Betty's willingness to embrace the LGBTQ+ community in the 1980' when a whole lot of other actors wouldn't have wanted to have anything to do with such a storyline as the LGBTQ + community wasn't widely accepted yet.

Her Other Achievements

She was recognized as a Kentucky Colonel, the highest honor from the Commonwealth of Kentucky.

As the saying goes, "TV is Betty White, and Betty White is TV." Having the Guinness World record for Longest TV Career for an entertainer, ranging from acting to hosting TV Shows, Betty is said to have had a strong impact on making the TV what it is today.

The Chairman and CEO of the Academy of Television Arts and Sciences, Frank Scherma, had told TODAY in an interview concerning Betty White, "You can almost say that she and television matured together at the same time." He went further to say, "And that medium was so new, the television medium was so new, she was in a position to do lots of different things, a little bit of everything. She was just a natural performer. She was just great at it."

"I think when you look at her, and you look at television, you realize that they grew up together and that the history of television was close to her growth in our business, which I think is extraordinary," Frank stated.

Another feat Betty attained in the TV Industry was the Sitcom show "Life with Elizabeth," which she had produced in the 1950s, a period when it wasn't expected or easy for a woman to do such.

Despite society's attitude toward encouraging racial discrimination in the early '90s, Betty wasn't found in such a circle. In 1954, it was noted that Betty still gave Arthur Duncan, a black tap dancer, a role on her show despite several backlashes. Her response to those who criticized her was even more hilarious as she said, "I'm sorry. Live with it." She even went further to give Duncan more screen time, although it wasn't long after that the show was canceled.

White broke another record as the first woman to win an Emmy award for hosting a game show or just men!

Her fellow legend in comedy, Carl Reiner, who is now late, had stated before about her, "A lot of us are here because she was there at the beginning. She set the standard. She set the way for many people."

Betty White: A Celebration

In December 2021, it was announced that Betty would mark her 100 years birthday with the release of a documentary movie about her titled "Betty White: 100 years young- A Birthday Celebration." The title was changed to "Betty White: A Celebration" after the celebrity's death on December 31, 2021.

It features interviews with many friends and famous Hollywood stars such as Ryan Reynolds, Tina Fey, Robert Redford, Lin-Manuel Miranda, Clint Eastwood, Morgan Freeman, Jay Leno, Carol Burnett, Craig Ferguson, Jimmy Kimmel, Valerie Bertinelli, James Corden, Wendie Malick, and Jennifer Love Hewitt.

The movie also features Betty's last tribute to her fans, recorded ten days before her death.

She was also featured in the cover story of people's magazine for January 2022, a newsstand publication, and a commemorative edition to celebrate the anticipated milestone.

Betty White A Celebration

http://allaboutbookseries.com/BettyWhiteACelebration

Betty White's Timeline

January 17, 1922- Betty White was born in Oak Park, Illinois.

1923- The White family moves to Alhambra, California

1939- Betty begins her career in the entertainment industry. She is just seventeen.

1941- Betty volunteers for the American Women's voluntary service.

1949- Betty begins co-hosting "Hollywood on Television" with Al Jarvis.

1951- Betty became one of the first women to be nominated for Emmy Awards "Best Actress" on television, competing with Judith Anderson, Helen Hayes, Gertrude Berg, and Imogene Coca.

1952- Betty becomes the host of "Hollywood on Television."

1952- Betty created Bandy productions alongside writer George Tibbles and Don Fedderson, a producer.

1952- Betty becomes the first woman to produce a sitcom

1952- Betty's sitcom "Life with Elizabeth" won a Los Angeles Emmy award.

1952- She began hosting the "Betty White Show."

July 1959- Betty made her professional stage debut in a week-long play, Third Best Sport, at the Ephrata Legion Star Playhouse, Pennsylvania.

1963- Betty married Allen Ludden.

1971- Betty began her advocacy for a better and improved animal welfare system.

1973- She became a cast member of the Mary Tyler Moore show.

1975- Betty was replaced as the commentator of the NBC Roses Parade.

1983- Betty became the first woman to win a Daytime Emmy Award in Outstanding Game Show Host for the NBC entry Just Men!

1983-1984- Betty played the role of Ellen Harper in "Mama's Family" and "The Carol Burnett Show."

1985- She got the role of Rose Nylund in the Golden Girls.

1986- Betty won Female Star of the year in the Golden Apple Award.

1987- Betty won the Funniest Female Performer in a TV Series.

1990- She won a Lifetime Achievement award in comedy.

1992- The golden girls ended when Bea Arthur left the show.

1992- Betty White stars in the "Golden Palace" alongside Rue McClanahan and Estelle Getty.

1995- Betty White became the Mayor of Hollywood.

1995- Betty White was inducted into the Television Walk of Fame.

1995- Betty won a Star on the Walk of Fame under the Hollywood Walk of Fame.

1996- Betty won an Emmy award for Outstanding Guest Actress in a Comedy Series, appearing on The John Larroquette Show.

2000- Betty won Funniest female Guest appearance in the TV Series Ally McBeal.

2004- Betty had a guest appearance on "The Practice" as Catherine Piper.

2005- Betty once again plays the role of Catherine Piper in "Boston Legal."

December 2006- She joined the cast of "The Bold and Beautiful," playing the role of Ann Douglas.

2007- Betty did a commercial for PetMed express, showcasing her love for animals.

May 2008- She had a guest appearance on "The Oprah Winfrey Show."

2009- Betty starred in "The Proposal" alongside Ryan Reynolds.

2009- She starred in the Mars campaign ad for the Super Bowl.

2009- She was awarded the Jane Goodall Institute Global Leadership Award.

May 8, 2010- Betty White hosted Saturday Night's Live, becoming the oldest person to host the show at 88.

June 2010- The actress joined the cast of "Hot in Cleveland," playing the role of Ella Ostrovsky.

2010- Betty won a Primetime Emmy Award for Outstanding Guest Actress in a Comedy Series.

2010- Betty White was inducted into the California Hall of Fame.

2010- Betty won a Lifetime Achievement Award.

2010- Betty established the Betty While Wildlife Fund through the Morris Animal Foundation.

2011- Betty White was nominated for a Primetime Emmy Award for Outstanding Supporting Actress in a Comedy Series

2011- Betty White won a screen actors guild for Outstanding Performance by a Female Actor in a Comedy Series.

2011- Betty starred in the Hallmark of Fame's presentation of "The Lost Valentine."

2011- Betty won a UCLA Jack Benny Award as a comedian.

2011- Betty won a Grammy Award for the audio recording of her book, *If You Ask Me, And of Course, You Won't.*

2012- Betty White won her second screen actors Guild for Outstanding Performance by a Female Actor in a Comedy Series.

2013- She changed her name to *Betty Purple* for a day to show her support for the lgbtq+ community by celebrating the spirit day, which is an anti-LGBTQ+ bullying awareness day.

2014- Betty gets a Guinness record as the female with the longest TV career by an entertainer.

2015- Betty White appeared on the 40th anniversary special of Saturday night's live.

2015- Betty White was given an honorary lifetime achievement award.

2015- She won TV Icon in the People's Choice Award.

2018- Betty White was crowned "The First Lady of Television" in a PBS documentary.

2019- Betty White plays the voice of Bitey White, a tiger in Pixar's *Toy Story 4*.

2021- Betty won a Lifetime Achievement Award under the Women Film Critics Circle Award.

December 31, 2021- Betty White dies; she's seventeen days from becoming 100 years.

January 17, 2022- Betty White: A celebration is released in theaters in the United States. It features the actress' last message to her fans.

January 31, 2022- "Celebrating Betty White: America's Golden Girl" will air on NBC and will later be available to stream on Peacock. It is a unique tribute to the actress.

References

General

https://en.m.wikipedia.org/wiki/Betty_White

https://youtu.be/r88MI16aTyA

Introduction

https://en.m.wikipedia.org/wiki/Betty_White

Early Childhood

https://en.m.wikipedia.org/wiki/Betty_White

https://youtu.be/Cw7KV_RRdyI

Career and Achievements

https://youtu.be/Cw7KV_RRdyI

https://youtu.be/rDcSqChFJ94

https://en.m.wikipedia.org/wiki/Betty_White

https://youtu.be/_o83aMEBFQs

Betty White's Emmy for The Mary Tyler Moore show

https://youtu.be/EeYUI08azWw

Betty White's 2015 Daytime Emmys Lifetime Achievement Award

https://youtu.be/n1D-d-MrHlk

Betty White's Screen Actors Guild Awards for lifetime achievement

https://youtu.be/dm940gD48WQ

70th Primetime Emmy Awards Celebration for Betty White

https://youtu.be/RfsA2Q6Jrec

Things you didn't know about Betty White

https://youtu.be/aKRvl_LJ-98

Betty White wins People's Choice Award

https://youtu.be/lLdD0dsUopg

Betty White's Guinness World Record

http://www.guinnessworldrecords.com/world-records/107740-longest-tv-career-by-an-entertainer-female

Betty White on the John Larroquette show

https://m.imdb.com/title/tt0616639/

Mary Tyler Moore show

https://televisionheaven.co.uk/reviews/the-mary-tyler-moore-show

Todd Milliner's speech about Betty White in Hot in Cleveland and Tribute

https://variety.com/2022/tv/news/betty-white-hot-in-cleveland-1235146378/amp/

Betty White's death

https://people.com/tv/betty-white-cause-of-death-revealed/?amp=true

https://people.com/tv/betty-white-the-golden-girls-and-hot-in-cleveland-star-dead-at-99/?amp=true

Betty White: A celebration

https://people.com/tv/betty-white-100-birthday-movie-special-will-move-forward-how-when-to-watch/?amp=true

https://www.hollywoodreporter.com/movies/movie-news/betty-white-a-celebration-movie-1235075184/amp/

Final Surprise Bonus

Hope you've enjoyed this biography of Betty White

We always like to give more than we get, so I'd like to give you one final bonus.

Do me a favor, if you enjoyed this book, *please* leave a review on Amazon.

It'll help get the word out so more kids can find out more about Betty White!

If you do, I'll send you one of my most cherished video collection – Free:

Ultimate Collection of Links to Betty White's YouTube Videos!

You won't be able to say you know Betty White until you watch these videos!

Here's how to claim your free videos:

1. Leave a review right away -

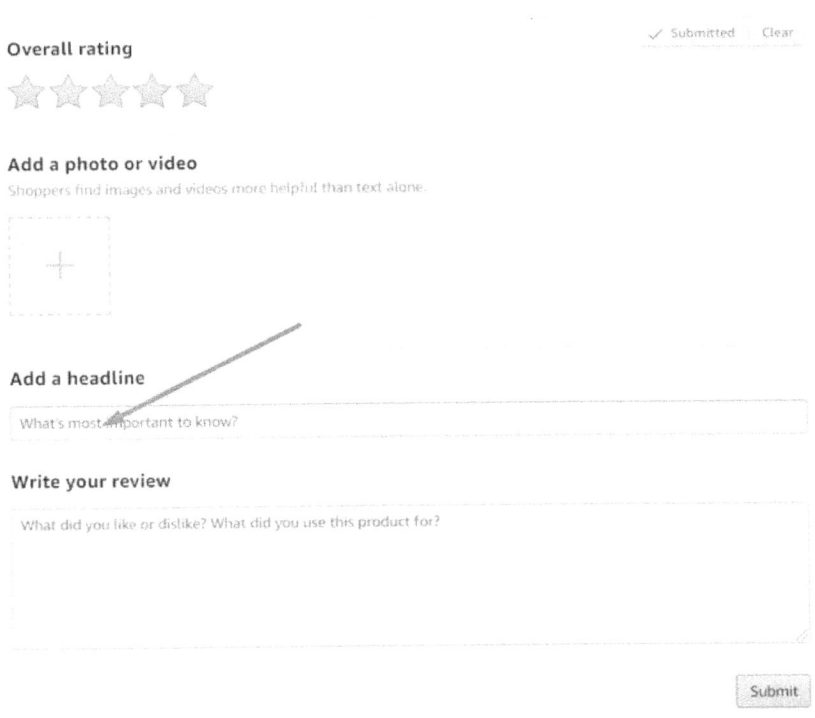

2. Send a screenshot of your review to: reviews@allaboutbookseries.com with the subject line: All About Betty White Review

3. Receive your free video collection – "Ultimate Collection of Links to Betty White's YouTube Videos! " – *immediately*!